A WALK IN PARADISE

SANTHOSH ANNABATTULA

ISBN 979-888555570-8

Dedicated to
Aparajitha Rokkam

Contents

About "Abstract Pain"

1. Abstract Pain 3

About "Au Revoir"

2. Au Revoir 7

About "In The Path Of Your Happiness"

3. In The Path Of Your Happiness 13

About "Journey To Freedom"

4. Journey To Freedom 17

About "Metamorphosis"

5. Metamorphosis 23

About "Road Less Traveled"

6. Road Less Traveled 27

About "Rower"

7. Rower 33

About "Story Of A Smile"

8. Story Of A Smile 37

About "The Liberation Song"

9. The Liberation Song 41

About "Woven From The Same Fabric"

10. Woven From The Same Fabric 45

About Team 47

About Community 49

About "Abstract Pain"

Describing the mental pain of a man who is seeking eternal peace, poet Santhosh Annabattula crafts his verses writing the thoughts of a fallen spirit filled with sorrow. "Abstract Pain" is a paradox stating that the pain within our minds is an abstract entity that could be eliminated even if our spirits are broken.

CHAPTER ONE

Abstract Pain

I stand on the threshold of pain
With the autumn rain for tears
Eyes behold the blurred horizon
In all its shades of grey

Days dissolve into oblivion
Time flies past in disdain
People move like puppets
Tied by strings of callousness

All that was once beautiful
Is buried under the ages
As the world crumbles inside
Shattering the wounded soul

Empty spaces grow everywhere
Bred by the seeds of isolation
Memories freeze the heart
Draining the last traces of hope

I stand on the threshold of pain
When nature sings in lament

I let go of my senses
And wait to embrace death.

About “Au Revoir”

Narrating the story of a lonely flower hoping to find a companion, poet Santhosh Annabattula writes about how the flower found his lover. However, as nature dictates, happiness is short-lived as his lover leaves soaring into the skies. In a tragic yet poetic way, the poem “Au Revoir” masterfully talks about how a lonely soul couldn’t resist but seek his lover throughout the final stage of his life.

CHAPTER TWO

AU REVOIR

Once there was a flower
Among many of his kind
Neither fragrant nor beautiful
But life blossomed in his spirit

Morning, noon and night
He waited with undying hope
For a companion to feel for
As time ticked in loneliness

She came from the sky above
Like a moving rainbow of colours
Weary and broken the butterfly was
She fell straight into his arms

He cared her back to health
With the warmth of a mother
He brought her back the smile
With the camaraderie of a friend

He listened to her enchanted
As she told stories of the world

He felt happiness like never before
As he came alive in her presence

With the wind back in her wings
She soared up into the sunlight
Happy and dancing the butterfly was
She charmed her way into his heart

The winds have changed course
Time rolled on with the clouds
She disappeared into the twilight
Leaving a trail of darkness behind

He looked on with a foolish hope
With every breath longing for her
All colour drained out from the world
As he sank to the depths of despair

The first rays of dawn roused him
He mustered all the spirit left
And broke away from his abode
To be blown into the wilderness

He looked for her everywhere
On earth, water and sky
He braved the sun and the rain
And slept under the stars

His search passing in vain
His strength and will failing
He drifted along with the wind
Only with blind hope by his side

Death was within reach
When he saw a silhouette
She rushed to his side
He felt warm in her lap

There was one thing left to say
For which he came all the way
He spoke, smiled and went quiet
"Au Revoir my love"

About “In the Path of Your Happiness”

Being mocked by forces beyond human spirit while being occupied in his pursuit of fulfilling his dreams, poet Santhosh Annabattula describes how Hope reached out to help him to stand against the odds. The poem “In the Path of Your Happiness”, talks about the light at the end of the tunnel just like the sunrise after a dark night. It mentions that with Hope along our side in our moment of need, we are unstoppable.

CHAPTER THREE

In the Path of Your Happiness

I was sitting on a lonely beach,
Building castles in the wet sand.
A nonchalant wave sweeps it away
Making a mockery of my dreams
I crumble down in despair,
Until a pair of hands help me,
To build it stronger this time.
I look up and see your smiling visage
And stare at your eyes in wonder
At how alike we both are
While a silent smile crosses my heart
Realizing that I'm not alone.
Many people we meet in life,
The wind which passes through everything,
Sings only in a special piece of wood
Every note of music flowing out of the alliance.
The moon is what but rock and stone
Until it is tenderly touched upon by light.
The sun and the rain seldom meet
But nature paints a rainbow whenever they do,

In joyous celebration of their togetherness.
You showed me there is a dawn
After every twilight; And that night
Is only a brief journey towards the light
You saw and woke up the butterfly,
Hidden inside the façade of a caterpillar.
Your thought is like the first drop of rain,
Heralding the shower of happiness.
Your warmth is shared by the first ray of dawn,
Which melts the darkness from the inside.
Your grace resembles a thousand candles,
A light in humble devotion to the lord.
Your voice is the sweetness,
In the lullaby of a doting mother.
Your friendship is the all-embracing sky,
Which distances can never split
In these times of fleeting promises,
Of shallow emotions and masquerades
You rise like the evening star so fair
Shining like a beacon of hope.
Is this all really you?
Or is this how I see you?
That is best left unanswered
For my mind is already made
I hope all my prayers
Will find a way to fulfil your wishes
For I will find bliss
Only in the path of your happiness.

About “Journey to Freedom”

Questioning anyone who is bound in the shackles of working their lives out, poet Santhosh extends his hand to join him in breaking free and relishing their lives forever. While questioning the reason behind leading such a life, the poet asks if such an existence is worthy after being gifted such a wonderful life by the Gods.

CHAPTER FOUR

JOURNEY TO FREEDOM

What have we become?
Cogs in the machinations of life
Puppets in controlling hands
Prisoners of our aspirations
Patients of order and restraint
Come fly with me my friend
On this journey to freedom.

When was the last time
You had time for yourself
When you stood at the brink of dawn
Against a dazzling sky and a warm sea
With the waves lapping against your feet
When you sipped a coffee
Losing yourself in the fumes of ecstasy
When you looked beyond your window
To feel the wind caressing your face
When you sang aloud uninhibited
When you danced in the rain
Splashing the water with your feet

When you followed a rainbow
When you had a date with the full moon
When you unleashed your senses
When you had all the time in the world
To walk alongside yourself
When was the last time?
When you expressed how much
You love your loved ones
When you gave a warm hug
When your hand found a friend's shoulder
When you kissed passionately
When you apologize whole-heartedly
When you confessed your deepest secrets
When you cried your heart out
Leaning over a caring shoulder
When you experienced the feeling
Of sleeping in your mother's lap
Of holding your father's hand
When you lost yourself in the moment
Relishing a blissful happiness
Because life is shorter than it seems.
When was the last time my friend?
That you were just yourself
When you shed those false pretenses
When you didn't give a damn
When you never cared about how you look
Or how you dressed and talked
When you became a child again
Following your instincts without regrets
When you took failures in a stride
When you laughed at your foolishness
When you took pride in your weaknesses
When you broke a rule just for the fun of it

When you actually enjoyed being idle
When you screamed out your resentment,
Shattering the barriers of silence.
When you last looked in the mirror,
And wondered how beautiful you are,
What an awesome creation you are!
When was the last time
You woke up a new morning and felt excited
About what the new day brings
About those new people you meet
About the new things you experience
When was the last time
You fully lived your life in the present
Come reflect with me my friend
On what we miss in life
Come fly with me my friend
On this journey to freedom!

About "Metamorphosis"

A lover fearing rejection expresses her feelings through her art. Conquering her fear and taking a leap of faith, she confesses her undying love and asks her soulmate about leading a life together. Santhosh Annabattula through the poem Metamorphosis shows that any pursuit is only as strong as the belief invested in it.

CHAPTER FIVE

Metamorphosis

A spirit is kindled within my body,
Long in waiting with an earnest hope.
Both deep and superficial at once,
It shakes me from my slumber of reality.

I become the tiny speck of dust,
Dancing in the beam of sunlight.
I become the wave of the ocean that,
Pounds its forceful fist on the shore.

I turn into the nonchalant rain cloud,
Teasing all the lands beneath with its shadow.
I drift along with the lightest of feathers,
And dropdown with melting snowflakes.

Until a sober voice echoes in my head
Chiding me to steady my wandering heart
But who doesn't fall for unbridled happiness
And the love I feel when I think about you!

How would you feel when I tell you this?
The force of it hits me hard at my insides

Doubt and fear interlace with my thoughts
I wait as moonlight stopped in its tracks,
Ready to take flight with a leap of faith
Across the darkest stretches of the night
Leaving all the questions for time to answer.

About "Road Less Traveled"

Pondering on "Who Am I?" poet Santhosh writes his thoughts and ideas explored. In his journey, the poet offers his view on society and education while mapping them to his question to find an answer. While the initial response seems to be that we are nothing more than meat, our thoughts seem to be the answer after a moment of reflection. However, in conclusion, the poet offers who we are in a unique way that defines what we have been doing since the beginning.

CHAPTER SIX

Road Less Traveled

It all begins with a question
"Who am I?"
Am I just a bundle of flesh and bones?
No. I'm something more than that,
Am I just a mind which thinks?
Or am I just a heart that feels,
Deep inside am I something more?

What is it that makes me?
People talk about a soul,
But have I ever really felt it?
So who am I? I have got past.
Am I a collection of memories?

I look hopefully towards the future
Am I defined by my emotions and feelings?
Or by my character, my personality, my traits,
Which I have built all over the years!

But am I really living the way I want?

I have been influenced by people
In that case, I am just one in a billion
People wear masks, they pretend, they act,

So am I acting too?
Am I living the life I really wanted?
And what is that life which I really wanted?
Will I ever know it?

And even if I know wouldn't it be influenced
By my upbringing and society!
So what is it which defines me?
The way I look at this world!

But isn't it a myopic vision,
Narrowed by knowledge and education,
I look only through a keyhole,
And pretend that I see the world.

What if I am alone in this world?
I am born alone, and I grow on my own,
With all my impulses and instincts,
Will I be myself then?

Will I be able to discover the real me?
So what is it which makes me?
Am I defined by my dreams?
We are so obsessed with our dreams

That we wish for reality to be the same.
We see the world with these dreamy eyes,
Which blurs the line between reality.
And the question lingers,

"Who am I?"

Deep down voice echoes
That I am just a traveller,
On the road to self-discovery.

About "Rower"

Writing about the life of a lonely rower, poet Santhosh talks about how different people repay the rower when he drops them on the other shore before returning to his true home, the river water, until sunset. The poem "Rower" illustrates the feelings of a rower on a sunny day.

CHAPTER SEVEN

ROWER

I am a rower
Living by my boat
Paddling through life,
Wading through the waters
Sometimes rough, sometimes smooth
I carry people as my own
Some on the shore, some lost in the water
I take them to safety
To the far bank ashore
I carry them with care,
Listening to their stories
Cherishing every moment together
I row against the current
Against wind and storm alike
To carry people as my own...

When I leave them ashore
Some bid a fond farewell
Some just give me a smile
Some nod and go on their way
And some never look back
But I do what I do best

And go back to the waters
With thoughts like ripples,
Many people I meet
Yet I am always alone
As no one stays behind.
I am a lonely rower
Paddling through life
Without ashore to reach
As the ripples ebb away
I retreat into the sunset
After a hard day's work.

About "Story of a Smile"

To be loved or to love are unparalleled feelings. Our life, decisions, perspective, and experiences are never the same again. What we love seems close to being a mythical artefact we adore caring about unendingly. "The Story of a Smile" by Santhosh Annabattula elicits one such experience of a lover free-falling into bliss, relishing the beauty of a smile.

CHAPTER EIGHT

Story of a Smile

It all starts with a twinkle in her eyes,
And I start free falling,
Hurling through space and time,
Where was the earth that stood beneath?
A gust of wind sends a shiver through me.

I see now a chuckle in her cheeks.
I inhale the air which she breathes,
And I am free-falling towards nothing,
I can feel neither happiness nor any pain,
Lost was I in a blissful state of transcendence.

It then forms a quiver on her lips,
Parting them ever so slightly.
My soul is drenched in the feeling,
Is this what happiness is, I wonder?
While I am free-falling,
How is the world going past in oblivion?

While I wait with bated breath.
Finally the smile blossoms on her visage,
Freezing time in its relentless tracks,

As though my whole life, my whole journey,

From the microcosm to the macrocosm,
Was leading me to this point.
I surrender to the sea of emotions,
As I die and am reborn every moment,
While I am free-falling,

Lost in a blissful state of transcendence.
All my senses come alive,
As her smile rings in my ears,
I am free-falling towards her,

Indeed love is the new gravity.

About "The Liberation Song"

Narrating the pain that forces us to let loose and be liberated, poet Santhosh Annabattula states that all of us hold ourselves until the threshold is crossed, and then hell shall be let loose, and with the intensity of a thousand suns, we shall reach our goal. The poem "The Liberation Song" expresses the desire for awakening to get the best of our potential.

CHAPTER NINE

The Liberation Song

Every nerve in the body throbbing to break free
Each drop of blood screaming in exasperation
When you become your own nemesis
The pain consuming you entirely
The darkness throttling your hope
Walls of steel closing all around
Shards of agony scarring your soul
Your own feelings ripping you apart
And your insides pleading for death
When life becomes terrifyingly long
World turning into a bleak nightmare
When you start drifting from yourself...

Then
You discover a voice among the debris
An instrument of expression...
You regain your failing senses
Taking refuge in your heart
When you become your own saviour
You stand up and fight back

A phoenix born from the ashes
With your passion by your side
Your belief showing you the light
Riding on the tide of your dreams
With the intensity of a thousand suns
Scorching everything in between
You claim what is rightfully yours
When you finally rise above life
And you become your own destiny.

About "Woven from the Same Fabric"

Writing about humanity, poet Santhosh Annabattula mentions how we all belong to the same family while being separated by boundaries set within our minds. Through Woven from Same Fabric, the poet talks about how the human spirit binds us together while stating it's our bonding that could ever complete us.

CHAPTER TEN

Woven from the Same Fabric

Look over your shoulder
For there is a friend waiting
To hold your hand in communion,
In the winding journeys of life
To turn every place you go,
A special space called home.
What brings us together?
We are what we are
Fallen leaves drifting with the wind,
Still clinging to the parent tree
Raindrops from the same cloud,
Flowing in unknown waters
Birds of the same nest,
Lost in the wilderness
Searching for an identity
Until we find someone
Who completes us!
We are but reflections
Mirroring each other
Parts of the same whole

Entwined like flowering creepers
Growing with each other
We are what we are
Distant stars in the sky
Spreading the same light.

What brings us closer?
Some bonds are made not in blood
Strangers yesterday, friends today
Separated by distances, united in spirit
To come alive in each other's company
We drift apart only to come together
Because we are meant to be.

About Team

1. ***Santhosh Annabattula***
   Poet

   Santhosh has been a member of the community since 2011 and he writes short stories & poems. His works can be accessed at writerspouch.com/profile/3

2. ***Pankaj Tottada***
   Photographer

   Pankaj has been a member of the community since 2015 and he has contributed numerous photographs. His contributions can be accessed at writerspouch.com/profile/13

About Community

Writers Pouch is an Indian community that commissions various works of different art forms. Encompassing creators, contributors, editors, proofreaders, reviewers, photographers, and illustrators, the organisation aims to create unique forms of art in every genre.

Established in 2009, Writers Pouch started by publishing short stories, essays and poems. Later on, the organisation even started releasing novelettes, novellas, novels, book series, & non-fiction.

The goal of Writers Pouch is to explore art uniquely and this is accomplished by commissioning a group of artists on every project. They are a home for all creative individuals who are striving to tell their stories or ideas creatively while holding on to their principles.

If you loved our works, visit our website at writerspouch.com to buy our other titles.

1. *I'm Your Loving Intern [2015]*
2. *Loving Intern [2016]*
3. *The Soul Snatchers [2016]*
4. *Broken Bonds [2017]*
5. *God's Council: The Four Auins [2017]*
6. *Your Loving Intern [2018]*
7. *Eternal Love [2019]*

About Community

[illegible]

9 798885 555708

Printed by Libri Plureos GmbH in Hamburg, Germany